The Future of AI: How Artificial Intelligence is Shaping Education, Productivity, and Everyday Life

A Beginner's Guide to Understanding AI, What is AI, Mastering Time Management, and Using AI Tools to Transform Your Future

Alex Harper

Contents

Foreword — v

1. WHAT IS AI, AND WHY DOES IT MATTER? — 1
2. PERSONAL PRODUCTIVITY BOOSTERS WITH AI — 6
   - Revolutionizing Task Management with AI — 6
   - Email Drafting, Meeting Notes, and Reminders — 7
   - Reducing Workload with AI Automation — 8
   - Time Management Enhanced by AI — 9
   - Real-Life Scenarios Where AI Boosts Productivity — 10
3. AI AND YOUR DAILY ROUTINE — 12
   - Smart Scheduling Using AI-Powered Calendars and Apps — 12
   - Simplifying Meal Planning and Grocery Shopping with AI — 13
   - Personal Assistants for Household Chores and Reminders — 14
   - Balancing Work-Life Routines Through AI Recommendations — 15
4. FINANCIAL EMPOWERMENT THROUGH AI — 19
   - Budgeting Made Easy with AI-Driven Tools — 19
   - How AI Helps with Investment Decisions and Market Analysis — 20
   - Automated Savings, Expense Tracking, and Bill Payment Management — 21
   - Expense Tracking with AI — 22
   - Case Studies of Individuals Optimizing Their Finances Using AI — 22
   - Practical Steps to Financial Empowerment with AI — 23
5. DECISION-MAKING SMARTER AND FASTER — 25
   - AI in Research and Analysis for Better Decisions — 25
   - Comparative Shopping: Getting the Best Deals with AI Assistance — 26

    Enhancing Creativity and Brainstorming with AI Tools   27
    AI for Planning Trips, Events, and Major Life Decisions   28
    Practical Steps to Smarter Decision-Making with AI   30

6. STAYING INFORMED AND EDUCATED WITH AI   31
    AI as a Personal Tutor for Learning New Skills or Languages   32
    Using AI to Stay Updated on News and Trends Tailored to Your Interests   32
    Customizing Your Knowledge Base with AI Tools   33
    Stories of Lifelong Learners Empowered by AI   34
    Practical Steps to Integrate AI into Your Learning Routine   34

7. OVERCOMING AI ANXIETY   37
    Common Fears About AI and How to Address Them   37
    Understanding AI's Limitations   39
    Building Digital Literacy to Use AI Responsibly   40
    Ethical Considerations for Using AI in Everyday Life   40
    Real-World Stories of Overcoming AI Anxiety   41
    Practical Steps to Overcome AI Anxiety   42

8. THE FUTURE OF AI IN EVERYDAY LIFE   44
    Emerging AI Trends and Innovations   44
    Potential Disruptions and Challenges   46
    Preparing for AI Advancements in Key Areas   47
    Case Studies of Future AI Applications   48
    Practical Steps to Prepare for the Future of AI   49

Appendices   51

Foreword

In an age where the rhythm of life grows ever more frenetic, technology has become both our salvation and our challenge. We are inundated with tools designed to streamline our existence, yet the paradox persists: the more gadgets we embrace, the more complicated life seems to become. Amid this whirlwind, artificial intelligence (AI) has emerged not as just another tool, but as a revolutionary force poised to transform the way we live, work, and think. This book, *AI for Everyday Life: Practical Tips to Save Time, Work Smarter, and Achieve More*, offers a beacon of clarity in the storm of digital possibilities.

When I first encountered AI in its most accessible forms—chatbots that could compose emails, apps that could track spending, and algorithms that curated my playlists—it felt like stepping into a science fiction novel. But like many, I was skeptical. Could this technology really simplify my life, or was it just another digital distraction? I asked myself the same questions many of you may be asking now: Is AI truly worth the hype? Is it safe? Is it for people like me who aren't programmers or tech-savvy engineers?

Foreword

The answers to these questions didn't come overnight. They unfolded as I began to experiment, cautiously at first, with AI tools. A virtual assistant helped me organize my chaotic work schedule. An app analyzed my spending habits and suggested ways to save money. Another tool streamlined my grocery shopping, ensuring I never forgot the milk. It wasn't long before I realized that AI wasn't a replacement for my effort or creativity; it was an amplifier. It freed me from the mundane, empowering me to focus on what truly mattered.

The beauty of AI lies in its accessibility. You don't need to be a tech wizard to benefit from it. You don't even need to fully understand the complex algorithms that power it. What you need is curiosity and a willingness to embrace change. This book is your companion on that journey, guiding you through the practical applications of AI in everyday life, demystifying its complexities, and helping you unlock its potential to save time, work smarter, and achieve more.

But let's take a step back. Why does this book matter now? The answer is simple: because AI is no longer a luxury or a novelty—it's a necessity. We live in a world where information overload is the norm, where balancing work and life feels like an impossible equation, and where time is the most precious commodity. AI offers solutions not in abstract, theoretical ways, but in tangible, actionable steps that anyone can implement.

What makes this book special is its approach. It doesn't ask you to become an AI expert. Instead, it meets you where you are, offering a user-friendly exploration of tools and strategies that can make a real difference in your daily life. Whether you're a busy professional looking to optimize your workflow, a parent juggling countless responsibilities, or a lifelong learner eager to explore new horizons, this book provides practical advice tailored to your needs.

The chapters ahead are a roadmap to empowerment. You'll learn what AI is and why it matters in ways that go beyond the buzzwords. You'll discover how AI can help you organize your day, manage your

Foreword

finances, and make better decisions. You'll explore how it can spark creativity, enhance your education, and even address some of the anxieties surrounding its use. Most importantly, you'll come away with the confidence to integrate AI into your life in ways that feel natural and effective.

One of the most inspiring aspects of this book is its emphasis on balance. AI isn't here to replace human ingenuity, empathy, or intuition. It's here to augment them. This isn't a story about surrendering control to machines; it's about reclaiming control of your time and energy. It's about making space for the things that truly matter—whether that's pursuing a passion, spending time with loved ones, or simply enjoying the quiet moments that too often slip away.

As you turn the pages of this book, I encourage you to approach it with an open mind and a sense of curiosity. Try the tools, implement the strategies, and see for yourself how AI can transform the way you live. Remember, this isn't just about learning to use technology; it's about discovering new possibilities for yourself and your future.

I've experienced firsthand how AI can turn the mundane into moments of creativity and efficiency. It has given me back hours of my day, helped me make smarter decisions, and even sparked ideas I never would have considered on my own. And while I am by no means an AI expert, I am a testament to the power of being willing to learn and adapt. If I can do it, so can you.

In a world where change is constant, one thing remains true: the tools we choose to embrace can shape the lives we lead. AI is one of those tools, and this book is your guide to using it wisely and well. So take a deep breath, dive in, and get ready to discover how AI can help you work smarter, live better, and achieve more.

>Welcome to the future.
>>Welcome to the possibilities.
>>Welcome to *AI for Everyday Life*.

Chapter 1
What is AI, and Why Does It Matter?

In the simplest terms, artificial intelligence (AI) refers to machines or systems that can perform tasks that typically require human intelligence. These tasks include problem-solving, decision-making, understanding natural language, and even recognizing patterns. While the concept of AI might sound futuristic, it's already woven into the fabric of our daily lives, from the recommendations you get on Netflix to the voice assistant on your smartphone. But what exactly is AI, and why is it so crucial for modern life? Let's dive deeper.

Introduction to Artificial Intelligence: A Simplified Explanation

At its core, AI is about creating systems that can process data, learn from it, and make decisions or predictions. There are two main types of AI:

1 Narrow AI: This is the AI we encounter most frequently. It's designed to perform specific tasks, such as recommending a song, answering a question, or recognizing faces in photos. Narrow AI excels at what it does but is limited in scope—your email spam filter is excellent at identifying unwanted messages, but it won't help you write a novel.

2 General AI: This is the theoretical concept of a machine capable of performing any intellectual task that a human can do. While this form of AI sparks fascination and fear in equal measure, it remains a concept for the future and isn't the focus of this book.

Imagine AI as a digital assistant that never tires, learns over time, and gets better at helping you as it processes more information. For example, when you use a ride-sharing app like Uber or Lyft, AI is working behind the scenes to match you with the nearest driver, calculate the best route, and adjust pricing based on demand. These processes happen so seamlessly that you may not even notice AI is at work.

The Current Landscape of AI in Personal and Professional Spaces

AI is no longer confined to tech labs or science fiction. It has infiltrated nearly every aspect of our lives, transforming how we work, communicate, and solve problems. Let's explore some areas where AI is making an impact:

1. Personal Spaces

- **Entertainment**: Streaming services like Netflix and Spotify use AI algorithms to analyze your viewing or listening habits and recommend content you're likely to enjoy. The more you engage, the better these systems understand your preferences.
- **Smart Home Devices**: Voice-activated assistants like Amazon Alexa and Google Assistant rely on AI to interpret your commands, whether you're setting a timer, controlling your lights, or asking for the weather forecast.
- **Health and Fitness**: Wearable devices like Fitbit and Apple Watch leverage AI to track your physical activity, monitor your heart rate, and provide insights into your health.

2. Professional Spaces

- **Customer Service**: Chatbots powered by AI handle inquiries, book appointments, and solve basic problems without human intervention. This reduces wait times and improves efficiency.
- **Recruitment**: AI tools analyze resumes, screen candidates, and even predict which applicants are most likely to succeed in a given role.
- **Data Analysis**: In industries like finance, marketing, and healthcare, AI systems process vast amounts of data to identify trends, anomalies, and opportunities faster than any human could.

These examples illustrate AI's versatility and its growing presence in both personal and professional domains.

Why Understanding and Using AI Is Essential in Modern Life

AI is no longer a luxury; it's a necessity. Here's why embracing AI is crucial:

1. Efficiency and Productivity

AI automates repetitive tasks, freeing up time for more meaningful work. Consider a business owner who uses AI-powered tools to schedule social media posts, manage inventory, and handle customer inquiries. By offloading these tasks to AI, they can focus on strategy and growth.

2. Better Decision-Making

AI analyzes data at a speed and scale beyond human capability, providing insights that inform smarter decisions. For instance, farmers use AI to monitor crop health, predict weather patterns, and optimize irrigation, increasing yields while conserving resources.

3. Staying Competitive

In today's fast-paced world, those who leverage AI gain a significant advantage. Businesses that adopt AI can innovate faster, adapt to market changes, and deliver personalized experiences that customers value.

4. Improved Accessibility

AI makes technology more accessible to diverse populations. Voice assistants help visually impaired users navigate devices, while AI-driven language translation tools break down communication barriers.

Real-World Example: In education, AI-powered apps like Khan Academy and Duolingo provide personalized learning experiences, adapting to each student's pace and skill level. This democratizes access to quality education, enabling people worldwide to learn new skills.

AI Misconceptions Debunked

Despite its benefits, AI is often misunderstood. Let's address some common misconceptions:

1. AI Will Replace All Jobs

While it's true that AI is automating certain roles, it's also creating new opportunities. For example, AI has revolutionized industries like data science, cybersecurity, and software development, creating jobs that didn't exist a decade ago. Moreover, AI tools often augment human workers rather than replacing them. A graphic designer using AI to generate ideas or a doctor using AI for diagnostic support is more productive, not obsolete.

2. AI Is Only for Tech Experts

Many believe AI is complicated and reserved for programmers or large corporations. In reality, tools like ChatGPT, Grammarly, and Canva are user-friendly and require no technical expertise. AI is for anyone willing to explore it.

3. AI Is Always Watching

Concerns about privacy are valid, but not all AI systems collect personal data. Many tools operate locally on your device, ensuring your information remains private. Understanding how AI works can help alleviate these fears and encourage responsible use.

4. AI Is Infallible

AI is powerful, but it's not perfect. Algorithms are only as good as the data they're trained on. Bias in data can lead to flawed outcomes, which is why human oversight remains essential.

Real-World Example: In 2018, a major retailer faced backlash when its AI-powered hiring system was found to favor male candidates over equally qualified women. The system had learned biases from historical hiring data. This highlights the importance of ethical AI development and vigilant monitoring.

Conclusion

AI is not a distant, mysterious technology; it's a practical tool that can simplify our lives, enhance our capabilities, and open doors to new possibilities. Understanding what AI is—and what it isn't—empowers us to embrace its potential responsibly. This chapter has laid the foundation for exploring AI's role in your personal and professional life. As we move forward, you'll learn how to leverage AI for productivity, creativity, and decision-making, transforming the way you live and work.

In the chapters to come, we'll break down specific use cases and provide actionable tips to help you harness AI's power. But for now, remember this: AI isn't about replacing what makes us human; it's about amplifying it. Welcome to the world of AI—your new partner in achieving more.

Chapter 2
Personal Productivity Boosters with AI

In today's fast-paced world, staying productive isn't just about working harder; it's about working smarter. Artificial intelligence (AI) offers tools and strategies to help you manage your time, streamline repetitive tasks, and focus on what truly matters. From organizing your day to reducing mental clutter, AI-powered solutions can transform how you approach productivity.

This chapter dives into the practical ways AI can become your personal productivity ally, offering actionable guidance and real-world examples to help you get started.

Revolutionizing Task Management with AI

Prioritizing Tasks and Staying Organized

AI excels at organizing complex information and helping you focus on what's important. Task management apps like Todoist, Notion, and Microsoft To Do now integrate AI to sort your tasks by priority, set reminders, and even suggest the best times to complete them based on your schedule.

Real-World Example: Imagine you're juggling multiple projects with overlapping deadlines. AI-powered apps can analyze your tasks, recognize overlapping time frames, and propose an optimized schedule. For instance, Notion's AI can help you break large projects into smaller, actionable steps and assign due dates automatically, minimizing the stress of manual planning.

Actionable Tip: Start by integrating an AI-powered task manager into your routine. Input your daily to-do list, and let the AI help you prioritize. Tools like Motion even adapt in real-time, rescheduling tasks if something unexpected comes up.

Email Drafting, Meeting Notes, and Reminders

Drafting Emails with AI

Writing emails can be time-consuming, but tools like Grammarly, ChatGPT, and even email platforms like Gmail are equipped with AI features that draft, edit, and suggest responses.

Real-World Example: Suppose you need to send a professional email to a client. Tools like Grammarly's tone detector or ChatGPT can help you draft a message that's clear, polite, and professional in seconds. Gmail's "Smart Compose" feature even suggests how to finish sentences, saving you precious minutes.

Actionable Tip: Experiment with AI writing tools for routine emails. Start by inputting key details and let the AI create a polished draft. Review it for accuracy and personalization, and you're good to go.

Taking Meeting Notes

AI tools like Otter.ai and Microsoft Teams can transcribe meetings in real-time, summarize key points, and even generate follow-up tasks.

Real-World Example: Imagine you're in a 90-minute brainstorming session. Instead of frantically scribbling notes, Otter.ai can transcribe the entire conversation, highlight action items, and email a summary to participants. You leave the meeting with a clear understanding and no missed details.

Actionable Tip: Use an AI meeting assistant to handle notetaking during your next meeting. Focus on the discussion while the tool captures everything.

Reminders and Follow-Ups

AI-powered virtual assistants like Google Assistant, Siri, and Alexa excel at setting reminders and nudging you to follow through.

Real-World Example: If you forget birthdays or routine chores, AI can help. For example, you can tell Alexa, "Remind me to call Mom on her birthday next Friday," and you'll receive a timely alert.

Actionable Tip: Synchronize your virtual assistant with your calendar to automate reminders for both personal and professional commitments.

Reducing Workload with AI Automation

Automating Routine Tasks

Automation is a cornerstone of AI productivity. Tools like Zapier and IFTTT allow you to connect different apps and automate workflows. For example, you can set up a "zap" to automatically save email attachments to a cloud folder or post new blog updates to your social media.

Real-World Example: A freelance writer uses Zapier to streamline client management. When a new client submits a form, Zapier automatically creates a Trello card, sends a welcome email, and schedules an introductory meeting. This eliminates hours of manual work.

Actionable Tip: Identify repetitive tasks in your workflow. Use tools like Zapier to create automation that connects your apps and simplifies your processes.

Streamlining File Management

AI tools like Google Drive and OneDrive offer intelligent file organization. They suggest where to store files based on your habits and even retrieve documents through natural language search.

Real-World Example: A small business owner uses Google Drive's AI-powered search to find contracts quickly. Instead of navigating folders, they simply type "John Doe contract from March 2023," and the file appears instantly.

Actionable Tip: Start using cloud storage with AI capabilities. Organize files with keywords, and let the system's AI help you retrieve them when needed.

Time Management Enhanced by AI

Time-Blocking and Scheduling

AI-powered calendars like Google Calendar and tools like Motion or Clockwise help you block time efficiently. They analyze your habits, suggest the best times for meetings, and even balance focus time with collaborative tasks.

Real-World Example: An executive uses Clockwise to manage their day. The app integrates with their calendar, automatically scheduling meetings and reserving uninterrupted blocks of time for deep work.

Actionable Tip: Enable smart scheduling in your calendar app. Block focus time daily and let the AI manage meeting requests around it.

Minimizing Distractions

AI can monitor your digital habits and provide recommendations to reduce distractions. Apps like RescueTime and Focus@Will analyze how you spend your time and suggest changes to improve focus.

Real-World Example: A student struggling with procrastination uses RescueTime to track screen time. The app identifies that they spend too much time on social media and recommends productivity-enhancing adjustments, such as limiting access during study hours.

Actionable Tip: Install a productivity-tracking app to understand where your time goes. Follow its suggestions to eliminate distractions.

Real-Life Scenarios Where AI Boosts Productivity

Case Study 1: A Busy Professional

Sarah is a project manager who juggles multiple deadlines daily. She uses Notion to manage her tasks and integrates it with Slack via Zapier. When a teammate updates a project, Sarah receives an automatic notification, saving her from checking multiple platforms. She also uses Otter.ai to transcribe client meetings and Grammarly to draft clear, professional emails.

Result: Sarah saves 10+ hours weekly, reduces stress, and meets deadlines effortlessly.

Case Study 2: A Small Business Owner

Tom runs a bakery and uses AI to simplify his operations. He automates inventory management with Square and schedules social media posts with Buffer. AI even helps him predict customer demand based on historical sales data, ensuring he never overbakes or underbakes.

Result: Tom improves efficiency, reduces waste, and grows his customer base.

Practical Steps to Implement AI for Productivity

1 Identify Your Pain Points: Start by listing tasks that feel repetitive or time-consuming. Whether it's managing emails, scheduling, or taking notes, there's likely an AI tool for the job.

2 Choose the Right Tools: Explore popular AI apps and platforms. For beginners, start with user-friendly options like Grammarly for writing, Google Calendar for scheduling, or Notion for task management.

3 Experiment and Iterate: Use AI tools consistently for a few weeks. Evaluate their impact on your productivity and adjust your approach as needed.

4 Stay Updated: AI tools evolve rapidly. Follow updates and new features to ensure you're using the latest capabilities.

Conclusion

AI isn't just about cutting-edge technology—it's about reclaiming your time and energy. By integrating AI into your daily routines, you can reduce workload, eliminate inefficiencies, and focus on what matters most. Whether you're a professional, student, or small business owner, the tools and strategies in this chapter can help you work smarter, not harder.

In the next chapter, we'll explore how AI can simplify your daily routine, from meal planning to household management, ensuring you make the most of every moment.

Chapter 3
AI and Your Daily Routine

Our daily routines are filled with repetitive tasks, decision fatigue, and competing demands on our time. Artificial intelligence (AI) has the potential to simplify and enhance these routines, enabling us to focus on what matters most. From managing schedules to streamlining household chores, AI tools are reshaping how we approach everyday life.

This chapter explores how you can integrate AI into your daily routine with practical, actionable advice and real-world examples. By the end, you'll see how small adjustments with AI can lead to significant improvements in efficiency, organization, and work-life balance.

Smart Scheduling Using AI-Powered Calendars and Apps

Keeping track of meetings, appointments, and deadlines can be overwhelming. AI-powered calendars like Google Calendar, Microsoft Outlook, and third-party tools like Motion and Clockwise can take the hassle out of managing your schedule.

. . .

How AI Calendars Work

AI scheduling tools analyze your preferences, availability, and priorities to optimize your calendar. They can:

• Suggest the best times for meetings based on your availability and that of other participants.

• Automatically block "focus time" for deep work.

• Reschedule overlapping or canceled appointments.

• Integrate with other apps like task managers, email, and project tools.

Real-World Example

Imagine you're a remote worker juggling meetings across different time zones. Tools like Motion can automatically adjust your schedule to accommodate time differences while ensuring you have dedicated time for tasks and breaks. Clockwise, on the other hand, can reorganize your day to minimize context switching, allowing you to stay focused.

Actionable Tip

Sync your calendar with an AI scheduling tool. Start by setting parameters like working hours, preferred meeting times, and focus blocks. Allow the AI to suggest optimal times for your activities, and review its recommendations.

Simplifying Meal Planning and Grocery Shopping with AI

Meal planning and grocery shopping can be time-consuming and mentally exhausting. AI tools are here to help, offering personalized meal recommendations, recipes, and streamlined shopping lists.

AI for Meal Planning

Apps like Yummly, Mealime, and Paprika use AI to recommend recipes based on your dietary preferences, available ingredients, and nutritional goals. Some apps even integrate with your grocery store's inventory to suggest meals using items currently on sale.

. . .

AI for Grocery Shopping

AI-powered platforms like Instacart, Amazon Fresh, and Walmart+ use algorithms to predict your shopping needs based on past purchases. They also suggest complementary products, saving you the trouble of making separate trips for forgotten items.

Real-World Example

Suppose you're trying to follow a healthy eating plan. Yummly can recommend a week's worth of recipes based on your caloric goals and dietary restrictions. It then generates a shopping list that you can send directly to an online grocery service like Instacart for delivery.

Actionable Tip

Choose an AI-powered meal planning app and set up your preferences. Spend a few minutes each week reviewing its meal suggestions and syncing your grocery list to a delivery service. Over time, you'll save hours while eating healthier.

Personal Assistants for Household Chores and Reminders

Personal assistants like Amazon Alexa, Google Assistant, and Apple's Siri are powerful tools for managing household tasks. These AI-driven systems can help with everything from setting reminders to controlling smart home devices.

Household Chores

AI assistants can integrate with smart devices to automate chores. For example:

- Use a smart thermostat like Nest to regulate your home's temperature.
- Program a robot vacuum like Roomba to clean your floors on a schedule.
- Automate laundry cycles with smart washing machines that send alerts when the load is done.

Reminders and Notifications

AI assistants are excellent for remembering birthdays, bill payments, and routine maintenance tasks like changing air filters or scheduling dentist appointments.

Real-World Example

A busy parent uses Alexa to create a daily routine. In the morning, Alexa turns on the lights, plays a wake-up playlist, and reads the day's weather. In the evening, it reminds them to prepare their child's lunch and prompts them to start the bedtime routine.

Actionable Tip

Set up an AI assistant in your home. Begin with simple tasks like setting timers or reminders. Gradually expand its use by connecting it to smart home devices and automating household chores.

Balancing Work-Life Routines Through AI Recommendations

Finding a healthy work-life balance can be challenging, but AI tools can help you create a more harmonious routine by analyzing your habits and suggesting improvements.

AI-Driven Insights

Wearable devices like Fitbit, Garmin, and the Apple Watch track your physical activity, sleep patterns, and stress levels. They use AI to provide actionable insights, such as when to take breaks, increase activity, or improve sleep hygiene.

Work-Life Integration

AI tools like RescueTime analyze your computer usage to identify patterns of productivity and distraction. They suggest when to step away from your desk, limit social media, or schedule time for relaxation.

Real-World Example

A software developer uses Fitbit to monitor their daily step count and sleep quality. Based on the data, Fitbit recommends a 15-minute evening walk to improve sleep and suggests scheduling breaks during long coding sessions to reduce fatigue.

Actionable Tip

Start using a wearable device or AI productivity tracker. Set goals for physical activity, screen time, and sleep. Follow the tool's suggestions to adjust your routine and track your progress.

AI-Powered Tools to Optimize Daily Routines

Here's a list of AI tools to help you get started:

1 Scheduling:

- **Google Calendar**: Suggests meeting times and blocks focus time.
- **Motion**: Dynamically reschedules tasks based on changing priorities.

2 Meal Planning and Shopping:

- **Yummly**: Personalized recipes and grocery lists.
- **Instacart**: Predicts shopping needs and suggests items.

3 Personal Assistants:

- **Amazon Alexa**: Integrates with smart home devices for seamless automation.
- **Google Assistant**: Offers contextual reminders and daily routines.

4 Work-Life Balance:

- **Fitbit**: Tracks activity, sleep, and stress.
- **RescueTime**: Provides insights into productivity and screen usage.

Case Study: Transforming a Routine with AI

Scenario: Maria, a full-time professional and parent, struggles to manage her daily schedule, meal planning, and household chores.

1 Scheduling: Maria integrates her Google Calendar with Motion, which schedules work meetings, blocks focus time, and sends reminders for her child's soccer practice.

2 Meal Planning: She uses Mealime to generate weekly meal plans based on her family's preferences. The app syncs with Instacart for grocery delivery.

3 Household Chores: Alexa reminds her to water the plants and start the dishwasher in the evening. A Roomba vacuum cleans the house while she's at work.

4 Work-Life Balance: Maria wears a Fitbit to track her sleep and stress. The app recommends a short yoga session in the evening to unwind.

Outcome: By delegating repetitive tasks to AI, Maria saves hours each week, reduces stress, and spends more quality time with her family.

Practical Steps to Implement AI in Your Routine

1 Start Small: Focus on one area, such as meal planning or scheduling. Gradually add more AI tools as you become comfortable.

2 Customize Settings: Tailor each tool to fit your preferences and lifestyle.

3 Evaluate Regularly: Assess how well each AI tool meets your needs and make adjustments.

4 Stay Informed: Keep an eye on new features and tools that could further simplify your routine.

Conclusion

AI is no longer a luxury—it's an essential part of modern life. By incorporating AI into your daily routine, you can reduce stress, save time, and achieve a better work-life balance. Whether it's managing your schedule, planning meals, or automating household chores, AI is here to make life easier. Start small, explore the tools that resonate with your needs, and watch your routine transform for the better.

In the next chapter, we'll explore how AI can empower your financial life, helping you budget smarter, save more, and even make informed investment decisions.

Chapter 4
Financial Empowerment Through AI

Managing finances can often feel daunting, with budgets to balance, expenses to track, and investments to monitor. Thankfully, artificial intelligence (AI) is here to simplify financial management, empowering individuals to take control of their money and make smarter decisions. AI-driven tools can help you automate budgeting, track spending, optimize investments, and save effortlessly—all while reducing the mental load.

In this chapter, we'll explore how AI can enhance your financial life, provide actionable steps to implement these tools, and highlight real-world success stories of individuals who've achieved financial empowerment through AI.

Budgeting Made Easy with AI-Driven Tools

Understanding AI-Powered Budgeting Tools

Traditional budgeting requires constant monitoring and manual adjustments, but AI simplifies the process by analyzing your spending habits, predicting expenses, and suggesting actionable steps to meet financial goals. Tools like **Mint**, **YNAB (You Need a Budget)**, and **PocketGuard** are leading the charge in AI-driven personal finance management.

• **Mint**: Tracks income, expenses, and savings automatically by linking to your bank accounts. It categorizes spending, identifies trends, and sends alerts when you're approaching your budget limits.

• **YNAB**: Uses AI to help you allocate every dollar you earn toward specific goals, promoting a proactive budgeting approach.

• **PocketGuard**: Analyzes your income and expenses to calculate how much you can safely spend each day while ensuring you meet your savings goals.

Real-World Example

Emily, a young professional, used to struggle with overspending on dining out. After linking her accounts to Mint, she noticed that dining took up 30% of her monthly budget. Mint's AI suggested a weekly dining limit and alerted her when she was close to exceeding it. Within three months, Emily reduced her dining expenses by 20% and redirected that money into savings.

Actionable Tip

Start with a free AI budgeting tool like Mint or PocketGuard. Set up your financial goals—whether it's paying off debt, saving for a vacation, or building an emergency fund—and let the tool guide your spending and saving habits.

How AI Helps with Investment Decisions and Market Analysis

AI in Investment Management

AI-powered platforms like **Betterment**, **Wealthfront**, and **Acorns** make investing accessible to everyone, regardless of expertise. These tools use sophisticated algorithms to:

• Analyze market trends.

- Create diversified portfolios tailored to your financial goals and risk tolerance.
- Automatically rebalance portfolios to optimize returns.

AI for Stock Market Analysis

For DIY investors, tools like **Morningstar Premium**, **Seeking Alpha**, and **Zacks Investment Research** use AI to analyze financial data, forecast market trends, and recommend stocks.

Real-World Example

James, a busy marketing executive, wanted to invest but didn't have time to research stocks. He signed up for Wealthfront, which used AI to design a portfolio aligned with his risk preferences. Over two years, Wealthfront's algorithm-managed portfolio outperformed James's previous DIY efforts, growing his investments by 12% annually.

Actionable Tip

Explore robo-advisors like Betterment or Wealthfront for hands-off investing. If you prefer a more hands-on approach, use AI-driven research tools like Morningstar to make informed decisions.

Automated Savings, Expense Tracking, and Bill Payment Management

Automated Savings with AI

Saving money can be challenging, but AI tools like **Digit**, **Qapital**, and **Chime** automate the process by analyzing your income and spending patterns. These tools determine how much you can afford to save and transfer that amount into a savings account.

- **Digit**: Automatically transfers small amounts into savings based on your spending habits. It even adjusts for upcoming bills to avoid overdrafts.
- **Qapital**: Allows you to set custom savings goals and rules, like

rounding up purchases to the nearest dollar and saving the difference.

• **Chime**: Automates savings by rounding up debit card transactions and transferring the difference into a savings account.

Expense Tracking with AI

Tools like **Expensify** and **Wally** simplify expense tracking by categorizing purchases, detecting irregularities, and even scanning receipts automatically.

Bill Payment Management

Late payments can damage your credit score, but AI tools like **Prism** and **Truebill** ensure you never miss a due date. Prism consolidates all your bills in one place and sends reminders, while Truebill negotiates lower rates for subscriptions and services.

Real-World Example

Samantha, a freelance writer, often forgot to pay her utility bills on time. After installing Prism, she set up automatic payments and reminders. Prism also identified that she was paying for a streaming service she no longer used, saving her $15 a month.

Actionable Tip

Download an AI-powered savings app like Digit or Qapital to automate your savings. Pair it with a bill management tool like Prism to ensure timely payments and eliminate unnecessary subscriptions.

Case Studies of Individuals Optimizing Their Finances Using AI

Case Study 1: Budgeting and Debt Reduction

Profile: Tom, a schoolteacher with $10,000 in credit card debt.

Challenge: Tom struggled to manage his monthly expenses while paying down debt.

Solution: Using YNAB, Tom created a zero-based budget and allocated every dollar toward specific goals. YNAB's AI highlighted unnecessary expenses, such as multiple streaming subscriptions. Tom redirected those funds to his credit card payments, cutting his debt in half within a year.

Case Study 2: Investment Growth

Profile: Anna, a recent college graduate with no investing experience.

Challenge: Anna wanted to start investing but felt overwhelmed by market complexities.

Solution: Anna signed up for Acorns, which automatically rounded up her daily purchases and invested the spare change in a diversified portfolio. Within two years, Anna built a $2,000 portfolio without even noticing the small daily contributions.

Case Study 3: Savings and Subscription Management

Profile: Jake, a software developer with inconsistent freelance income.

Challenge: Jake found it hard to save consistently and often overspent during high-income months.

Solution: Jake used Digit to automate savings and Truebill to manage subscriptions. Truebill flagged a gym membership Jake forgot to cancel, saving him $50 monthly. Digit helped him build an emergency fund of $5,000 over two years.

Practical Steps to Financial Empowerment with AI

1 Start with Budgeting: Choose a tool like Mint or YNAB to get a clear picture of your finances. Categorize expenses and set realistic goals.

2 Automate Savings: Use apps like Digit or Qapital to save money effortlessly. Set a goal, such as building a rainy-day fund or saving for a vacation.

3 Invest Smartly: Sign up for a robo-advisor like Betterment for long-term investing. If you're interested in stocks, use AI-powered research tools for data-driven decisions.

4 Track and Manage Expenses: Use apps like Expensify or Truebill to monitor spending and eliminate unnecessary costs.

5 Set Up Bill Reminders: Avoid late fees by using Prism or your bank's AI assistant to automate payments and receive notifications.

Conclusion

Financial empowerment is within reach for anyone willing to leverage AI tools. Whether you're managing a tight budget, investing for the future, or simply looking to save more, AI offers practical solutions that simplify and streamline the process. By automating routine tasks and providing personalized insights, these tools free you from financial stress and help you achieve your goals.

In the next chapter, we'll explore how AI can enhance decision-making, from comparing products and services to planning trips and tackling life's big choices. Get ready to become a more informed and confident decision-maker!

Chapter 5
Decision-Making Smarter and Faster

Making decisions is a cornerstone of daily life, whether it's choosing what to buy, how to approach a project, or where to go on vacation. The sheer number of choices we face can lead to decision fatigue, but artificial intelligence (AI) offers tools to simplify the process, enhance creativity, and improve outcomes. By leveraging AI's capabilities, you can make smarter, faster decisions in personal and professional contexts.

In this chapter, we'll explore how AI can assist with research, comparison shopping, brainstorming, and even major life planning. Through practical examples and actionable tips, you'll discover how to transform decision-making into an efficient and empowering process.

AI in Research and Analysis for Better Decisions

How AI Enhances Research

One of AI's greatest strengths is its ability to process vast amounts of information quickly and accurately. Whether you're researching a

product, analyzing data for work, or seeking insights for a personal project, AI can:
- Summarize complex information.
- Highlight key trends and insights.
- Provide data-driven recommendations.

Tools to Try:
- **ChatGPT or Bing AI**: Use these tools to ask detailed questions and receive concise, relevant answers.
- **WolframAlpha**: Ideal for technical, mathematical, and scientific queries.
- **Tableau**: For data visualization and trend analysis in professional settings.

Real-World Example

Sarah, a marketing manager, used ChatGPT to research emerging trends in her industry. Instead of spending hours reading articles, she asked for a summary of current best practices in digital marketing. With this information, she presented a strategic plan to her team in record time.

Actionable Tip

When starting a new project or making a significant decision, use an AI tool to gather and summarize information. Pair it with a tool like Tableau or Excel for deeper analysis if needed.

Comparative Shopping: Getting the Best Deals with AI Assistance

AI for Price Comparisons

AI-driven shopping tools help you find the best deals by comparing prices across retailers, monitoring discounts, and even predicting future price drops. Some of these tools include:
- **Honey**: A browser extension that finds and applies coupon codes at checkout.
- **CamelCamelCamel**: Tracks Amazon prices and sends alerts for price drops.

- **Google Shopping**: Uses AI to compare product prices across multiple sellers.

AI for Personalized Recommendations

AI can also provide recommendations tailored to your preferences, ensuring you find products that meet your needs and budget.

Real-World Example Jack wanted to buy a new laptop for work. By using Honey, he discovered a 15% discount coupon for a top-rated model. CamelCamelCamel also alerted him to a $200 price drop, saving him both time and money.

Actionable Tip

Before making a purchase, use a price-tracking tool to monitor discounts. For major purchases, set alerts to notify you when the price drops to your desired range.

Enhancing Creativity and Brainstorming with AI Tools

AI for Idea Generation

AI excels at sparking creativity, helping you brainstorm ideas, and refining concepts. Tools like **ChatGPT**, **Jasper AI**, and **Notion AI** can generate suggestions for:
- Business strategies.
- Creative writing.
- Marketing campaigns.
- Personal projects, like event planning or home design.

AI for Refining Ideas

Once you have a rough concept, AI tools can help refine and expand it. For instance, if you're brainstorming a social media campaign, AI can suggest catchy slogans, hashtags, or content ideas.

Real-World Example Linda, an entrepreneur, used Jasper AI to brainstorm taglines for her new eco-friendly skincare brand. Within minutes, she had a list of creative options that aligned with her brand's values. She also used ChatGPT to outline a social media content calendar, saving hours of work.

Actionable Tip

Use an AI tool like ChatGPT or Jasper for your next brainstorming session. Start with a broad question or prompt, and refine the results until you land on something actionable.

AI for Planning Trips, Events, and Major Life Decisions

Trip Planning with AI

Planning a trip involves choosing destinations, booking flights, and finding accommodations. AI simplifies this by:
- Suggesting destinations based on your preferences.
- Comparing flight and hotel prices.
- Recommending itineraries.

Tools to Try:
- **Google Travel**: Combines AI insights with user reviews to recommend destinations, activities, and accommodations.
- **Hopper**: Predicts the best times to book flights and hotels for maximum savings.
- **Kayak Explore**: Helps find budget-friendly travel options based on your starting location.

Real-World Example Emma and her family wanted to plan a vacation but didn't know where to start. Using Google Travel, they received personalized destination suggestions. Hopper helped them book flights at the lowest prices, and ChatGPT provided a tailored itinerary based on their interests in outdoor activities and historical sites.

Event Planning with AI

AI tools like **Evite** and **Canva** make event planning seamless by automating tasks like:
- Sending invitations.

- Designing event materials.
- Generating checklists for planning and execution.

Real-World Example Daniel used Canva to design invitations for his wedding and ChatGPT to draft a wedding timeline. With everything organized, he felt confident and stress-free leading up to the big day.

Making Major Life Decisions with AI

Major life decisions—such as buying a home, changing careers, or pursuing further education—require careful consideration. AI tools can help by:
- Providing data-driven insights (e.g., real estate trends or job market analysis).
- Offering personalized recommendations based on your goals and constraints.
- Running simulations to evaluate different scenarios.

Tools to Try:
- **Zillow**: For analyzing real estate options.
- **LinkedIn Learning**: For exploring new career paths.
- **Mint**: For understanding financial implications of major decisions.

Real-World Example After years in the corporate world, Rachel considered a career change. She used LinkedIn Learning to explore new skills and ChatGPT to research potential roles in her desired field. These tools helped her transition confidently into freelance consulting.

Actionable Tip

For your next big decision, break it into smaller questions and use AI to gather insights on each. Tools like ChatGPT or Google can help you evaluate options and weigh pros and cons.

Practical Steps to Smarter Decision-Making with AI

1 Identify Your Goal: Define what you're trying to achieve, whether it's finding the best deal, planning an event, or making a career decision.

2 Choose the Right Tool: Match your goal with an appropriate AI tool. For research, use ChatGPT or Google Bard. For shopping, try Honey or CamelCamelCamel. For creativity, explore Jasper or Canva.

3 Iterate and Refine: Start with a broad query or concept and refine it based on the AI's suggestions. For example, use ChatGPT to draft an outline, then tweak it to fit your specific needs.

4 Cross-Verify: Always verify important recommendations or insights from AI tools with reputable sources, especially for major life decisions.

5 Take Action: Use the insights and recommendations to make an informed decision. Follow through with confidence, knowing AI has saved you time and provided clarity.

Conclusion

AI is a powerful ally in decision-making, offering speed, clarity, and creativity to help you navigate choices both big and small. Whether you're brainstorming ideas, finding the best deals, or planning life events, AI simplifies the process and enhances your confidence. By integrating AI tools into your decision-making routine, you can reduce stress, save time, and make choices that align with your goals.

In the next chapter, we'll explore how AI can support lifelong learning and personal growth, enabling you to stay informed and continuously improve your skills. Get ready to unlock your full potential!

Chapter 6
Staying Informed and Educated with AI

In the digital age, staying informed and continuously learning are essential to personal and professional growth. AI has emerged as a transformative force in education and knowledge acquisition, offering personalized learning experiences, curated news, and tailored insights that align with individual interests and goals. From mastering a new language to staying up-to-date on global events, AI tools make lifelong learning accessible, efficient, and engaging.

This chapter explores how AI can revolutionize the way you learn, grow, and stay informed. Through detailed examples and actionable advice, you'll discover practical ways to harness AI for self-improvement.

AI as a Personal Tutor for Learning New Skills or Languages

How AI Enhances Learning

Traditional education often follows a one-size-fits-all approach, but AI adapts to your pace, preferences, and learning style. AI-powered platforms like **Duolingo**, **Khan Academy**, and **Coursera** provide:

- Customized lessons tailored to your proficiency.
- Real-time feedback to reinforce understanding.
- Motivation through gamification and progress tracking.

Real-World Example

Carlos, a sales manager, wanted to learn Spanish to better communicate with clients. Using Duolingo, he practiced daily with bite-sized lessons. The AI-powered platform adjusted difficulty levels based on his progress, and within six months, he was holding conversations confidently.

Actionable Tip

Set a clear learning goal, such as mastering a language or improving a skill. Use an AI tool like Duolingo for language learning or Khan Academy for academic subjects. Dedicate 15–30 minutes daily to build consistency.

Using AI to Stay Updated on News and Trends Tailored to Your Interests

Curated News Feeds

AI-powered news aggregators like **Feedly**, **Flipboard**, and **Google News** help you stay informed without sifting through irrelevant articles. These tools use algorithms to:

- Recommend articles based on your reading history and preferences.
- Filter out sensational or biased content.

- Summarize news to save time.

Real-World Example

Emma, a digital marketer, uses Feedly to track trends in her industry. The AI-driven platform aggregates articles from marketing blogs and websites, delivering daily updates directly to her dashboard. This allows her to stay ahead of competitors without spending hours searching for information.

Actionable Tip

Sign up for a news aggregator and customize your feed to focus on topics that matter most to you. Schedule a specific time each day to review the updates and avoid information overload.

Customizing Your Knowledge Base with AI Tools

AI for Self-Paced Learning

Platforms like **Notion**, **Obsidian**, and **Roam Research** use AI to help organize and recall information efficiently. These tools allow you to:

- Create a personal knowledge base with interconnected notes.
- Use AI to summarize articles or research papers.
- Generate ideas and insights based on your notes.

Real-World Example

David, a university student, uses Notion to organize his class notes. The AI assistant in Notion helps him create summaries of lengthy readings and provides suggestions for related topics to explore. This system has improved his understanding and retention of complex concepts.

Actionable Tip

Choose an AI-powered note-taking app and start building your knowledge base. Use its features to summarize key points from books, articles, or lectures, and revisit your notes regularly for deeper understanding.

Stories of Lifelong Learners Empowered by AI

Case Study 1: Language Mastery

Maya, a world traveler, used AI to learn multiple languages. She started with Duolingo for foundational vocabulary, then advanced to **Babbel** for conversational practice. By combining these tools with AI-powered translation apps like **Google Translate**, Maya was able to communicate fluently during her trips to Europe and Asia.

Case Study 2: Career Advancement

John, a graphic designer, wanted to stay competitive in his field. He used AI-powered platforms like **LinkedIn Learning** and **Skillshare** to learn motion graphics. The AI on these platforms recommended personalized courses based on his existing skills and career goals, helping him land higher-paying freelance gigs.

Case Study 3: Staying Ahead in Business

Sophia, an entrepreneur, relied on AI to monitor market trends and customer behavior. Using tools like **MarketMuse** and **BuzzSumo**, she gained actionable insights that helped her develop targeted marketing campaigns and grow her business by 30% in a year.

Practical Steps to Integrate AI into Your Learning Routine

1 **Define Your Learning Goals**: Identify what you want to achieve, whether it's mastering a skill, learning a new language, or staying informed about industry trends.

   2 **Choose the Right Tools**:
   ○ For skills: Platforms like Coursera or LinkedIn Learning.

- For languages: Duolingo, Babbel, or Rosetta Stone.
- For news and trends: Feedly or Flipboard.
- For organizing knowledge: Notion or Obsidian.

3 Set a Schedule: Dedicate a specific time each day or week to learning. AI tools often allow you to set reminders and track progress to keep you accountable.

4 Leverage AI Insights: Use features like personalized recommendations and progress tracking to make the most of your learning experience.

5 Review and Reflect: Regularly revisit your notes and insights. AI-powered tools can help you connect dots between ideas and reinforce learning.

The Role of AI in Lifelong Learning

AI isn't just a tool for acquiring new skills; it's a companion in lifelong learning. By adapting to your needs and offering tailored guidance, AI empowers you to:
- Stay competitive in a rapidly evolving job market.
- Explore new hobbies and interests.
- Make informed decisions based on curated, reliable information.

Conclusion

AI has revolutionized the way we stay informed and educated, offering personalized, efficient, and engaging ways to learn and grow. Whether you're a student, professional, or curious individual, AI tools provide the support you need to achieve your goals and expand your horizons. By integrating AI into your learning routine, you can unlock your full potential and embrace lifelong learning with confidence.

In the next chapter, we'll address common fears and anxieties about AI, exploring its limitations, ethical considerations, and strategies for using it responsibly. Let's demystify AI and build a relationship with technology that benefits everyone!

Chapter 7
Overcoming AI Anxiety

The rise of artificial intelligence (AI) has brought remarkable opportunities but also sparked anxiety and fear. Concerns about job displacement, privacy, ethical dilemmas, and the technology's rapid advancement can feel overwhelming. However, understanding AI's limitations, addressing misconceptions, and learning to use AI responsibly can transform fear into empowerment.

In this chapter, we'll explore common AI-related fears, debunk myths, and offer actionable guidance for building digital literacy and ethical awareness. By the end, you'll be equipped to navigate the AI revolution with confidence and control.

Common Fears About AI and How to Address Them

1. Fear of Job Displacement

One of the most prevalent concerns is that AI will replace human jobs, leaving millions unemployed.

- **Reality Check**: While AI will automate certain tasks, it will also create new opportunities. For example, roles in AI development, data analysis, and ethical AI oversight are growing. Additionally, AI often complements human skills rather than replacing them entirely.

• **Real-World Example**: In the healthcare industry, AI tools like IBM Watson assist doctors by analyzing medical records and suggesting treatment plans. Rather than replacing doctors, these tools help them make faster and more accurate decisions.

• **Actionable Tip**: Focus on skills that AI cannot easily replicate, such as creativity, emotional intelligence, and complex problem-solving. Platforms like LinkedIn Learning offer courses to upskill in areas where human expertise remains irreplaceable.

2. Fear of Privacy Violations

AI often requires large datasets to function effectively, raising concerns about data privacy and misuse.

• **Reality Check**: While some AI applications involve data collection, many tools operate locally on your device or use anonymized data. Understanding how your data is used and opting for privacy-focused tools can mitigate risks.

• **Real-World Example**: Signal, an AI-powered messaging app, prioritizes privacy by using end-to-end encryption and avoiding data collection. Similarly, DuckDuckGo is a search engine that doesn't track user activity.

• **Actionable Tip**: Review the privacy policies of AI tools you use. Opt for platforms with transparent data practices and enable privacy settings to minimize data sharing.

3. Fear of AI Bias

AI systems can inherit biases from the data they're trained on, leading to unfair outcomes.

• **Reality Check**: Bias in AI is a real challenge, but awareness and responsible design can reduce its impact. Developers are increasingly prioritizing ethical AI practices and transparent algorithms.

- **Real-World Example**: A hiring AI developed by a major tech company was found to favor male candidates due to biased training data. After identifying the issue, the company revamped its dataset and implemented checks to ensure fairness.
- **Actionable Tip**: Advocate for transparency in AI tools, especially in critical areas like hiring or lending. If you're a developer, focus on building diverse datasets and conducting rigorous bias audits.

4. Fear of Losing Control

Sci-fi narratives often depict AI as a runaway force, leading to fears that we may lose control over the technology.
- **Reality Check**: Current AI operates within defined parameters and lacks independent agency. Human oversight remains integral to AI systems.
- **Real-World Example**: Autonomous cars use AI to make driving decisions, but human drivers can still override the system in emergencies. Similarly, AI chatbots follow predefined rules and cannot act outside their programming.
- **Actionable Tip**: Learn how AI tools work and set boundaries for their use. Understanding the technology will help you maintain control and use it responsibly.

Understanding AI's Limitations

1. AI is Not Truly Intelligent

AI excels at pattern recognition and data analysis, but it lacks human qualities like intuition, creativity, and empathy. For example, while AI can generate artwork, it doesn't "understand" art in the way humans do.

2. AI Relies on Data

AI's performance depends on the quality of its training data. Poor or biased data can lead to inaccurate outcomes, making human oversight crucial.

3. AI Has Narrow Focus

Most AI tools are designed for specific tasks. For example, a language model like ChatGPT can assist with writing but won't help you manage your finances.

Actionable Tip: Use AI for tasks it excels at—automation, analysis, and pattern recognition—while relying on human judgment for nuanced or ethical decisions.

Building Digital Literacy to Use AI Responsibly

1. Learn the Basics of AI

Understanding how AI works will demystify the technology and reduce anxiety. Free resources like Coursera's "AI for Everyone" by Andrew Ng provide a beginner-friendly introduction.

2. Stay Informed About AI Ethics

AI ethics involves ensuring fairness, transparency, and accountability in AI systems. Follow organizations like the Partnership on AI to stay updated on ethical practices.

3. Experiment with AI Tools

Hands-on experience can build confidence. Start with user-friendly tools like Grammarly for writing or Google Lens for visual searches to see AI's practical benefits.

Actionable Tip: Dedicate an hour each week to learning about AI through online courses, articles, or podcasts. Experiment with one new AI tool each month to familiarize yourself with its potential.

Ethical Considerations for Using AI in Everyday Life

1. Be Mindful of Data Sharing

Before using an AI tool, consider whether it requires access to sensitive information. Opt for tools that prioritize privacy and minimize data collection.

2. Use AI for Positive Impact

Focus on applications that align with your values. For example, use AI to reduce your carbon footprint (e.g., apps like Oroeco) or support education and accessibility.

3. Advocate for Responsible AI

Support companies and initiatives that prioritize ethical AI development. If you work in tech, contribute to creating fair and inclusive systems.

Actionable Tip: Start a conversation about ethical AI in your community or workplace. Share resources and insights to encourage responsible adoption.

Real-World Stories of Overcoming AI Anxiety

Case Study 1: Embracing AI in Healthcare

Dr. Anna, a physician, initially feared that AI would devalue her expertise. However, after attending a workshop on AI in healthcare, she began using diagnostic tools to analyze patient data. These tools helped her make faster, more accurate diagnoses, enhancing her practice and patient outcomes.

Case Study 2: Addressing Privacy Concerns

Mark, a small business owner, was hesitant to use AI tools due to privacy concerns. After researching secure options, he adopted AI-powered accounting software with robust encryption. The tool streamlined his operations while protecting sensitive financial data.

Case Study 3: Navigating Bias

Sophia, a recruiter, was skeptical about using AI for hiring. By working with a diverse team to audit the AI system, she ensured it provided fair recommendations. This experience transformed her perception of AI as a tool that could enhance, rather than hinder, diversity.

Practical Steps to Overcome AI Anxiety

1 Educate Yourself:
- Take introductory courses on AI.
- Follow reputable sources like OpenAI or MIT Technology Review.

2 Start Small:
- Use simple AI tools for everyday tasks, like organizing your schedule or tracking expenses.
- Gradually expand to more advanced applications as you gain confidence.

3 Ask Questions:
- If you're unsure about an AI tool, research its features and limitations.
- Seek transparency from developers and companies.

4 Stay Critical:
- Evaluate AI recommendations critically.
- Combine AI insights with your judgment to make informed decisions.

5 Engage in Conversations:
- Discuss AI concerns with peers, colleagues, and experts.
- Share experiences to demystify the technology and build collective understanding.

Conclusion

AI anxiety is natural in the face of rapid technological change, but it doesn't have to hold you back. By educating yourself, addressing misconceptions, and using AI responsibly, you can turn fear into empowerment. Remember, AI is a tool designed to assist,

The Future of AI: How Artificial Intelligence is Shaping Education, ...

not replace, human abilities. With the right mindset and resources, you can embrace AI as a valuable partner in achieving your goals.

In the next chapter, we'll explore the future of AI in everyday life, examining emerging trends and preparing for innovations that will further shape our world. Get ready to step confidently into the future!

Chapter 8
The Future of AI in Everyday Life

Artificial intelligence (AI) is evolving rapidly, and its potential to reshape daily life is staggering. While we've already seen how AI can simplify tasks, enhance productivity, and empower decision-making, the future holds even more transformative possibilities. From healthcare to education, and entertainment to environmental sustainability, AI advancements promise to revolutionize how we live, work, and interact with the world.

In this chapter, we'll explore emerging AI trends, potential disruptions, and innovations that could redefine everyday life. By understanding these developments and preparing for the future, you can position yourself to thrive in an increasingly AI-driven world.

Emerging AI Trends and Innovations

1. Hyper-Personalized Experiences

AI is advancing toward creating hyper-personalized experiences that cater to individual preferences and needs. From shopping to entertainment, AI will adapt more intelligently to users.

• **Example**: Imagine a streaming platform like Netflix recommending not just movies but curating entire themed evenings, complete with meal delivery options and playlists that match your mood.

• **Future Potential**: Retailers could use AI to predict your needs before you know them, such as suggesting groceries based on your fridge's inventory (via smart appliances).

2. Conversational AI 2.0

AI-driven chatbots and virtual assistants are becoming more sophisticated, offering human-like interactions and understanding complex queries.

• **Example**: Future virtual assistants may not only schedule appointments but also negotiate prices, manage travel arrangements, and provide emotional support by analyzing tone and sentiment in conversations.

• **Future Potential**: These tools could evolve into "life assistants" capable of coordinating every aspect of your day.

3. AI in Healthcare

AI will play a growing role in preventative care, diagnostics, and personalized medicine.

• **Example**: Wearable devices like Apple Watch and Fitbit already use AI to monitor health metrics. In the future, they could predict medical conditions before symptoms appear.

• **Future Potential**: AI-powered home diagnostic tools could allow individuals to test for illnesses and receive instant, accurate recommendations for treatment or further testing.

. . .

4. Autonomous Systems

Self-driving cars, drones, and robots will become increasingly common, transforming transportation and logistics.

• **Example**: Autonomous vehicles like Tesla's cars are already navigating city streets. The future might bring door-to-door delivery robots or autonomous air taxis.

• **Future Potential**: Cities could redesign infrastructure to support autonomous systems, reducing traffic congestion and emissions.

Potential Disruptions and Challenges

1. Ethical and Privacy Concerns

As AI becomes more integrated into everyday life, ethical issues around data collection, surveillance, and bias will become more pressing.

• **Example**: Smart cities may use AI to optimize energy use and traffic flow, but such systems could also track citizens' movements, raising concerns about privacy.

• **Actionable Tip**: Advocate for transparency and accountability in AI systems. Support policies that prioritize privacy and ethical design.

2. Job Market Shifts

AI will automate repetitive tasks, potentially displacing jobs in some industries while creating opportunities in others.

• **Example**: Factory workers might face job losses due to automation, while demand for AI specialists and engineers grows.

• **Actionable Tip**: Future-proof your career by focusing on skills that AI cannot easily replicate, such as creativity, leadership, and emotional intelligence.

. . .

3. Digital Divide

Not everyone will have equal access to AI tools, potentially widening gaps in education, healthcare, and economic opportunity.

• **Example**: Rural areas or underfunded schools may lack the infrastructure to benefit from AI-driven educational tools.

• **Actionable Tip**: Support initiatives that promote digital equity, ensuring that AI benefits are accessible to all communities.

Preparing for AI Advancements in Key Areas

1. Healthcare

AI will transform healthcare delivery, making it more proactive and patient-centric.

• **Example**: AI algorithms could analyze your medical history and wearable device data to recommend personalized health plans.

• **Actionable Tip**: Invest in wearable health technology to monitor your health proactively. Stay informed about telemedicine and AI-powered health platforms.

2. Education

AI-driven tools will make education more adaptive, accessible, and engaging.

• **Example**: Virtual tutors could provide personalized learning experiences, while AI in classrooms could assist teachers in identifying students' strengths and weaknesses.

• **Actionable Tip**: Explore online courses and platforms that use AI to tailor learning experiences, such as Coursera or Khan Academy.

3. Entertainment

AI will continue to shape how we consume and create entertainment.

- **Example**: AI-generated content, such as music or films, could offer personalized experiences for viewers, with plotlines that adapt based on user input.
- **Actionable Tip**: Experiment with AI-powered creative tools like DALL-E for art or AIVA for music composition to explore your own creative potential.

4. Environmental Sustainability

AI will play a crucial role in combating climate change and promoting sustainability.

- **Example**: AI-powered tools can optimize energy grids, manage resources, and track deforestation using satellite imagery.
- **Future Potential**: Smart homes could use AI to reduce energy consumption by predicting your habits and optimizing appliance usage.

Actionable Tip: Adopt smart home technologies that use AI for energy efficiency. Support businesses and initiatives focused on using AI for environmental sustainability.

Case Studies of Future AI Applications

Case Study 1: Smart Cities

Singapore is pioneering smart city initiatives using AI to manage traffic flow, reduce energy use, and ensure public safety. Autonomous buses and predictive maintenance systems for infrastructure are just a few examples of how AI is shaping urban life.

Case Study 2: AI-Powered Agriculture

Farmers in India are using AI tools like Microsoft's FarmBeats to monitor soil health, predict weather patterns, and optimize irrigation.

This leads to higher yields and reduced waste, addressing food security challenges.

Case Study 3: Personalized Learning

In Finland, schools are integrating AI to provide individualized lesson plans for students, ensuring that each learner progresses at their own pace. This approach is closing achievement gaps and enhancing engagement.

Practical Steps to Prepare for the Future of AI

- **1 Stay Informed**:Follow AI news and trends through trusted sources like MIT Technology Review or OpenAI blogs. Take online courses to deepen your understanding of emerging technologies.
- **2 Adopt Early**: Experiment with cutting-edge AI tools to understand their capabilities and limitations. Upgrade your home or workplace with AI-powered systems to stay ahead of the curve.
- **3 Focus on Lifelong Learning**:Embrace continuous learning to adapt to changing industries and technologies.Develop skills in AI-related fields like data analysis, programming, or ethical AI design.
- **4 Advocate for Responsible AI**:Support policies and organizations promoting ethical AI development.Educate others about AI's benefits and challenges to foster informed discussions.
- **5 Invest in AI-Driven Solutions**:Explore AI tools that align with your goals, such as health monitoring devices, productivity apps, or creative platforms.Consider investments in AI-driven companies or projects that focus on sustainability and innovation.

Conclusion

The future of AI is full of promise, with advancements poised to improve nearly every aspect of daily life. By staying informed, embracing AI-driven tools, and advocating for ethical development, you can ensure that these innovations work for you and your community. The key is to remain adaptable, proactive, and informed as AI continues to evolve.

As we conclude this book, remember that AI isn't just a tool for productivity or convenience—it's an opportunity to shape a smarter, more connected, and sustainable world. The future is bright, and with the right mindset and resources, you're ready to embrace it. Welcome to the next chapter of human potential, powered by AI.

Appendices

Appendix A: Glossary of AI Terms for Everyday Users

Understanding the language of AI is crucial for navigating the tools and concepts discussed in this book. Here's a glossary of common AI terms:

- **Algorithm**: A set of instructions or rules that a computer follows to perform a task. AI algorithms are used to process data and make decisions.
- **Artificial Intelligence (AI)**: The simulation of human intelligence in machines, enabling them to perform tasks such as learning, problem-solving, and decision-making.
- **Automation**: The use of technology to perform tasks without human intervention, often through AI.
- **Bias**: A distortion in AI output caused by flawed or imbalanced training data.
- **Chatbot**: An AI-powered program that interacts with users via text or voice, simulating human conversation.
- **Data Training**: The process of teaching an AI system by

exposing it to large datasets so it can learn patterns and make predictions.
- **Deep Learning**: A subset of machine learning that uses neural networks to analyze data in layers, mimicking the human brain.
- **Machine Learning (ML)**: A type of AI that enables systems to learn and improve from experience without explicit programming.
- **Natural Language Processing (NLP)**: A branch of AI focused on enabling machines to understand, interpret, and respond to human language.
- **Neural Network**: A series of algorithms modeled after the human brain that allows AI to recognize patterns and solve complex problems.
- **Predictive Analytics**: The use of AI to analyze current data and predict future outcomes.
- **Robo-Advisor**: An AI-driven tool that provides financial advice or manages investments.
- **Supervised Learning**: A type of machine learning where AI is trained on labeled data, meaning the input and desired output are provided.
- **Unsupervised Learning**: A machine learning approach where AI identifies patterns and relationships in data without labeled examples.
- **Virtual Assistant**: AI programs like Alexa or Siri that perform tasks and answer questions through voice or text commands.

Appendices

Appendix B: Recommended AI Tools and Apps

Here's a curated list of AI tools and apps categorized by their purpose:

Productivity
- **Notion AI**: Enhances note-taking, task management, and brainstorming.
- **Grammarly**: Improves writing by offering grammar and style suggestions.
- **Otter.ai**: Provides real-time transcription for meetings and interviews.

Financial Management
- **Mint**: Tracks budgets, expenses, and savings.
- **YNAB (You Need a Budget)**: Helps users create zero-based budgets.
- **Betterment**: A robo-advisor for investment management.

Learning and Education
- **Duolingo**: AI-powered language learning with gamification.
- **Khan Academy**: Offers personalized learning in a variety of subjects.
- **Coursera**: Provides courses with AI recommendations based on interests.

Creativity
- **DALL-E**: Generates images based on text descriptions.
- **Jasper AI**: Assists with writing content for marketing, blogs, and more.
- **AIVA**: Composes music tailored to your preferences.

Health and Wellness
- **Fitbit**: Tracks health metrics with AI-driven insights.
- **MyFitnessPal**: Uses AI to recommend diet and exercise plans.
- **Headspace**: An AI-powered meditation app.

Shopping and Deals
- **Honey**: Finds and applies coupon codes automatically.

Appendices

- **CamelCamelCamel**: Tracks Amazon price history and alerts for drops.
- **Google Shopping**: Compares prices across multiple retailers.

Home and Lifestyle

- **Alexa/Google Assistant**: Manage smart home devices and get reminders.
- **Roomba**: AI-powered robotic vacuum for home cleaning.
- **Nest Thermostat**: Adjusts home temperature based on patterns.

Appendices

Appendix C: Troubleshooting Common Issues with AI Tools

AI tools are powerful, but they're not perfect. Here are common issues users face and how to resolve the

1. Tool Isn't Responding or Crashing

• **Cause**: The app may need updates or your device may lack sufficient resources.

• **Solution**:

  ○ Check for app updates in your device's app store.

  ○ Restart your device and try again.

  ○ Ensure your device meets the app's system requirement.

2. Inaccurate Results or Recommendations

• **Cause**: AI tools rely on data and may produce errors if the data is incomplete or biased.

• **Solution**:

  ○ Provide more specific inputs or refine your queries.

  ○ Check the tool's settings to see if preferences can be adjusted.

  ○ Verify results with additional sources if accuracy is critical.

3. Privacy Concerns

• **Cause**: Some AI tools collect and store data, raising privacy issues.

• **Solution**:

  ○ Review the tool's privacy policy and data usage practices.

  ○ Enable privacy settings where available.

  ○ Use privacy-focused alternatives if necessary.

4. Difficulty Integrating with Other Apps

• **Cause**: Compatibility issues between AI tools and existing systems.

• **Solution**:

  ○ Check for third-party integrations or plug-ins.

  ○ Use automation platforms like Zapier or IFTTT to connect apps.

5. Subscription or Cost Issues

Appendices

- **Cause**: Some AI tools have hidden fees or premium features.
- **Solution**:
  ○ Review pricing plans carefully before subscribing.
  ○ Start with free trials to evaluate the tool's value.
  ○ Opt for free alternatives if cost is a concern.

6. Overwhelming Notifications or Alerts

- **Cause**: AI tools can bombard users with frequent updates or suggestions.
- **Solution**:
  ○ Adjust notification settings to prioritize important alerts.
  ○ Mute or disable notifications temporarily during focus time.

7. Tool Lacks Customization

- **Cause**: The tool may not align with your unique needs.
- **Solution**:
  ○ Explore advanced settings or features for customization.
  ○ Provide feedback to developers; many AI tools are regularly updated based on user input.
  ○ Consider switching to a more customizable alternative.

These appendices serve as your quick reference for understanding AI terms, finding the best tools, and resolving common issues. With this knowledge at your fingertips, you're ready to navigate the AI-powered world confidently and effectively.

www.ingramcontent.com/pod-product-compliance
Lightning Source LLC
LaVergne TN
LVHW050026080526
838202LV00069B/6932